To Sherry
and
Jerry,

You have both been such a crucial part of giving me opportunities to find myself. "Maple Molly Brown" is in here directly because of you. I hope this brings you joy and pride, as you have given me.

Love,
Jon

#22

Lost Eel Questions

Poems by Jon Freeland

Stubborn Mule Press
Devil's Elbow, MO

Copyright © Jon Freeland, 2021
First Edition: 1 3 5 7 9 10 8 6 4 2
ISBN:978-1-952411-76-2
LCCN: 2021946423

Author photo: Jon Freeland
All rights reserved. No part of this publication may be reproduced or transmitted in any form or by any means, electronic or mechanical, including photocopying, recording or by info retrieval system, without prior written permission from the author.

Acknowledgments:

Special thanks to the Osage Arts Community, to John D., Mark, Tony, Zophia, Ed, Eva, Agnes, Jason R., Jason M., John C., Tim, Damian, Matt, and so many more. There really isn't a way for me to name every way all of you have been there with me. It makes me almost afraid to name people, in case I leave people out. Please know I hold your faces forever. Thank you to Stephen, Suzanne, and my Open Mic crew at Gumbo Bottoms. I also want to give special gratitude to Daphne – all I wanted out of that whole thing was to help people find their voice, and it's been a special pleasure watching people realize the fact that you're absolutely amazing.

TABLE OF CONTENTS

Family Tree / 1

Go-home Time / 3

He is. / 4

Motel Sick / 5

Hypertrophy: When You Spot Me / 6

not not / 7

The Ordinary Blossom Special / 8

Remarkable / 10

Montreal / 11

Flower Wall / 13

Lights and Loud Noises / 14

The Last Place / 16

Murmur / 17

Ironic / 19

Pygmalion / 21

The Rest Stop / 22

Laughtershocks / 25

For All the Holidays Ever Regretted / 26

Untitled / 27

Mountain Time / 28

West, to Fake California, MO / 30

Our Zone / 31

Seizer / 32

Call Away / 35

Wife* / 36

The Wolf Who Cried Boy / 37
Scotch Blankie / 38
The Life of a Sideways Sunflower / 39
Who Pays Your Heartbeat Bill? / 41
Eidolon / 42
Maple Molly Brown / 45
Ein Bier Bitte / 47
Rule of Thumb / 49
These Lyrical Bones / 50
The Wound / 52
The Charge of Laurens, 1782 / 54
Magnum Opus / 56
Puerto Rico / 58
Silence, Patience, Struggle / 59
Lockwork / 60
The Eel Question / 61

Thank you to my parents, Jon and Robin, who may not always have agreed with my decisions, but decided to let me find out for myself. I have eternal gratitude for my wife and my best friend. Joanna, very few people could have weathered me the way you have. Where I burned to fight, you always offered me healing water. I have a chance at being a whole person because you patiently want that for me. Vicky, you believed in my growth enough to give me chances to be beside you and have always pursued more with me. Our fire together has defiantly created where it would seem that we should burn out. 350+ poems seems like a lot now – I'm looking forward to where we end up. To Mat: this book very appropriately starts with you and me struggling together, creating pain which is at the very least our decision and under our control when we face so much which is outside of us every day. I would have no one else to stand beside.

To my sister, Cass: I have never seen anyone meet a challenge the way you do. Watching you find yourself has given me a much needed blueprint for finding myself. To my brother, Ian: we are siblings coming out of the small-mindedness of others. Do you think they ever imagined what giants we would become? It doesn't matter, really – we've done it together. Ali, you are entirely too young to grasp what is here now, but some day this will serve as something else for you to explore, as you have always been keen to curiously do. Loren and Rose, you have both only gotten to see the surface of my love for you both. You may never understand it, but that won't change how it grows every day. Grey, this life complicates family endlessly, but always know that I choose you and I'm glad to be Dad.

-JF

Lost Eel Questions

Family Tree

Brothers in effort
shifting piles of history
from the back of a borrowed bed,
heaving shared sweat, wounded wood, torn limbs:
glistening bodies reflected
in blue fiberglass.

We looked up at each other
and he exclaimed,
"Man, you're covered in cuts."

I trace the red road
half way from watch to elbow.
"Yep, got a good one here."

"And another on your side."

"A little pain is the fun part,"
and I can feel him look at me differently.
The liquid track marks
are poetry he knows by
trying heart despite
wounded mind.

"How are you so strong? You're one tough son of a bitch."
He doesn't know I've spent all day
sowing pieces of my body

knowing they'll never be his soul
hoping to grow another bruised plot
another row of useful scars
a garden I grew to be like him
with him another minute.

You want me to avoid the pain,
but it is our xylem
and I am a vine,
invasive, destructive, binding;
snap me in one place and find
I've grown in five others
because space and time
has only ever taken away,
forcing me to decide while breaking
what is mine by where I'm needed.

When they plant me,
I want to be the story
only those who are there
get to read.

Go-home Time

It's 16:35
walking out of Boone Med
and I spy the half moon
hiding in the sky
about a cloud
like when we were kids
trying to stuff into the cupboard
nearing the count of ten

then waiting silently
as it becomes an
imaginary laboratory
inventing, evading expectations.

He is,

and the worst part: he loves it.

He wants to jump on top of cubicle desk
and see if the dust supports him.

He wants to climb cracked stone and live on clay tiles
waiting for you to check the roof.

He wants to move in the mirror until his flesh looks less
like body and more like sex.

He wants to take your eyes, juice the why,
pry off the shaker top with nail or necessary tooth,

and make why-not angels
while there's everything to lose.

Motel Sick

Check out of what is expected.
Cheap overnight veneer.

If you could see the morning,
you'd say I have changed.
But that is to maintain
that I've lost something
when I've really gained

the ability to look past the words and the form
and realize that I deserve to burn down.

I am built to cut a hole
through every surface around
and walk in the aftermath,
calculating the relationship between
sound and signal, absence unceasing,

releasing the reasons why
someone should turn my light out.

Hypertrophy: When You Spot Me

When you see muscles
what is your first thought?

"That's pretty damn hot!"
"Obviously not compensating..."
"I wonder what keeps them motivated?"
"It's not for me, and even if it was, where would I start?"

Funny enough, I thought it began in bed,
where you hit bottom and I had struggled to stay on top.
We made something neither one of us could keep up with,
taken all our best and worst and every ounce of remaining
    energy,
leaving us spent.
The bed didn't shrink; we both drew closer to the opposite edges,
disgusted with ourselves and expecting the same of each other.

Until one day I walked in on you
nursing your sliver of space
and said, "I don't fit, but if you scoot just a bit
I'll know you want me." And you did.
So with every tissue, I've taut my body
to lean into you so that the only
way you'll need to know how hard I work
is by how much I grow.

not not

I live on the precipice
of giving everything up
if I let anyone down.

The way I have survived
my own onslaught
is to not even try.

Do you have any idea
how hard it is to not not try?

The Ordinary Blossom Special

> *I'm still learning to love the parts of myself that no one claps for.*
> ~Rudy Francisco

Anyone who knows me
knows I need data, feedback.

It's kinda hard to read,
"love you for YOU"
without a sarcastic Popeye
the sailor swing of the arm
and eye-popping
"aCtUaLlY, wHy DoN't YoU
lEaRn To Be HaPpY wItH
wHo YoU aRe?"

The answer is in when
I was 13 at the family reunion.
Aunts, uncles, cousins,
me and my new violin.
"Play Devil Went Down to Georgia!"
"Play Turkey in the Straw!"
"Play Orange Blossom Special!"

I watched the smiles fade
from their faces
as I replied, "No,"
wasting my gift,
useless.

The truth is:
it's easier choosing to fail
than to fail when you demand success.

Instead,
give me the moment you didn't expect.

Give me the fifth grader who kicked me in the legs so hard in soccer that I spun sideways twice, bruised for a week, and then was the talk of third grade for a month.

Give me the campaign where you needed a body and got one that will walk, talk, stress, and learn to code SRT because you asked for anyone in quiet frustration.

Give me the open mic where you expected rhythm and got action.

Give me every reference you ever spoke;
if I don't get the joke,
I will be it.
That's why I'm always a minute
or two to the goog
before I've responded
or I go way too far
and now it's ruined;

because in your grin
or even your chagrin,
at least I'm YOUR joke.

Remarkable

If this is failing,
I want to be the red pen
so I can feel your hand again.

Montreal

The grass is green,
as cold as it's been
and covered in leaves.

You were in springs
fresh with energy
like late night common
staring parties,
sweet as honeymoon
before spoonful of cinnamon.

But comment never new
and slowly
don't call me
Shirley
was once again true.

Deep fountain whimsies
said more than you
excusing from the food court
unfinished pizza in hand,
unfinished words in anger,
unfinished afternoon
rain still lingering,
twinkling off the cement:

the vibrations inside fingers
clutching an unfinished end.

The grass is green,
as cold as it's been
and covered in leave.

Flower Wall

Sidelines
to
Side-frowns
decide how
the wall flowers
seed the floor:

with hopes of loneliness—

a wayward glance,
imagined kiss...
the simplicities
often misinterpreted.

I look at you.
I like you.
I care for you.
I love you.
I hate you.
I miss you.

With pockets full of petals,
you watch the others fall,

then hide behind your hands where
they can't see you at all.

These hands make up the flower wall.

Lights and Loud Noises

When seeking sustained thrill, we look to the
lights and loud noises.

Over the big top (for now, it's on bottom),
the acrobats amaze as they dive through fiery hoops
of certain doom.

The people stand and gawk, bumping into backs,
inconvenienced, hurling curses.

What an affront!

Look! There's a couple on a ride…the woman screams
until the ride stops.
What a sight! What a sound.

"Save for the lights and loud noises,
where would the excitement be found?"
they eagerly ask the ring master of tasks.
"Oh, what's next?! What's in store for us?"

He answers as he always does,
"one dead. One wishing he was."

The face of his wife locked in eternal grimace,
he has wrapped his life around a light pole

like the pin-stripe of his suit,
the one he wore only yesterday when
lights and loud noises
had been such an entertaining display.

The Last Place

Missing you
is an exercise
in atrophy,
the only contest
I've ever won
and felt worse
then better
because you wanted
the loser.

Murmur

Whispers led to silence that
soft, loving curses
have known since our brazen days.
"Though appraised to be worthy of life,
all that is glitter does not gold."
Instead, it grows old
and loses its sheen to the
keening of the knife,

~

the wail brought forth to sunder
the welcoming of
an inkling, the blink of black
on red and blue video screen:
the herald of the penniless plight.
Precious pressure is
NO man's treasure, but he keeps
it for all his nights.

~

What follows is walk-sleeping;
silence is season
where work combines bland and loud:
a foul which may last a lifetime.
But I'd still die of young age
pacing in a cage,
like the tigers of false Spring,
lost to the sublime.

~

If all the new-found ones are
little angels, this
world will fashion its demons…
…and I hide one. Because of this, I am called
to preserve my enemy, willingly;
so few would undo
their own thread of existence -
it is killing me.

Ironic

Have you ever cared about something enough to kill it?
Picked flowers die fast;
it's about control and the moment.

Read today we are made of stars,
hearing naturelust in Damon Albarn's sweet Lou Reed
   refrain:

"Oh Lord, forgive me
Some kind of mixture
Some kind of gold
It's got to come and find us
All we are is dust."

FEeling birth among burning bodies,
Iron alone, black to the eye
until oxygen runs red.
Maybe we are blood fascinated
because it's the closest our atoms come to cosmic home.

How do we expect forever
when all we do is made to explode?

I knew it when Keenan
said monsters were surrogates
for necessary tragedy.

I knew it when Herbert cautioned through Muad'dib
that control and killing are degrees,
that violence is the transfer of energy.

Face cast off beveled glass
and for a moment I wonder
if I'm my anxiety's anxiety,
if self-improvement is simply a serial thought killer.

Pygmalion

Her, ivory is lovely and heavy,
so she focuses on the bone.
I am dreaming, burning yearning
loving life she hates to own.

{And I, whisper sharing}

Nightmares are perishable
and cannot keep outside of sleep.

Spirits never speak allowed
unless you seek them wanting.

Haunting becomes impossible
the moment after we come real

{Kiss Anyway}

from quiet nooneliness;
it is worth the weight to feel.

The Rest Stop

If I could draft a book of life,
it would be a choose your own Aventador,
a child's eye for acceptance and return,
grace and design,
and the freedom of the road.
In short: just cross the line in your own time.

In long:
if better were a letter
he'd written to himself
and stashed away beneath
the pencils, protractor
imperfectly ruled,
divided by compass and the dust
of a repurposed Swisher Sweets box,
I'd still have lost it in the move.

Hungry hands nudge needily,
the sweets of sticky fingers just
out of grasp,
out of sight;
memory might bleed,
her features fading into
something I miss, hastily
written down because momentum
is how I keep my moments
a zero-sum game,
progress and the same.

Does it have to be a balancing act?
Or did emotion mask the growing pain
of Evalution too fast for sinew,
the tendoncy to floor the gas
and feel it burning through vein lines
producing 1020 break horsepower?
If I can do 60 in 2.3, how fast have I done 32?

Too fast to stop
until we put our hands up.
Every stroke combusted and combined
like I love you fingers finding
each other drunk on contact,
head on laminate bar staring at legs,
watching lights and music dance
in spilled Bud Light and ignoring the rest.

But it's not repose if he must
recompose so he doesn't decompose.
It's recompense for his constant
offense and it doesn't make sense
that I long so much if I belong.

Now I really do be like that, sometimes.
Like is less lacking, and slowed
to park in the swing low
and contemplate of offering
yet, still managing
to mix the language
where it's too weird for the everyman
and too visceral for the laureate.

I know so many who create
and I want to
and I can, too,
but maybe less goes to waste
if my contribution is to listen;
laugh with all my lungs;
cry with all my joy;
watch in wonder;
give applause
a place
to rest.

Laughtershocks

There they were, minding their own business; they're
    so serious
when thunder bellows like cookie sheets
or tin roofing galvanized against rain...
but it came from...BELOW!
Body waves crest
through chest crust
and they are sorely pressed
to keep their focus!

The first priority is to find fault.
There is no time for mirthquakes
but a perfect chance to hurl complaints
at bellybutton epicenter shaking
the cubicle zirconium setting,
fighting like office siblings.
After all, we are family.

Could there be gratitude
after such magnitude?

For All the Holidays Ever Regretted

Because you are here,
the last year has taught me about
the value of the last year.

You know my compulsion
to compare

so holidays imply being holier
than the others.

I feel that's unfair

when I spend every second
of every minute
of every hour
of every day
of every year

on you, learning that holy is not a day
to feel less or do more,

that heilig is the healthy whole, to pick out
the common and render clear:

because you are here, the value
of the last year.

Untitled

Each of our children
begin without names
until we Rob them
of their potential.

I don't like titles.
Maybe, that's why mine
are bold and underlined
to separate the necessary
signposts from my essence,
concealed messages
not simply stolen.

Labels never purchased
the courage to be selfless
or selfmore, even selfsame.
Alloud mercurial insidety
is mad for simplicity.

I won't let you understand
without holding late in my hand
and making chase until underfall.

Then, I'll give you all the space in underland.

Mountain Time

I grew up near them,
fascinated with their peaks and slopes,
size immaterial in distance,
capped and contrasted with cracks and snow
and somehow, I slowly forgot over time
what they are but never lost the lust to close the range.

I think I've made them wherever I go
to replace the backdrop of lost home.

I remember the distinct feeling of moving, flat and wet,
not saltsweet mist but foreign breath
like the wild had been snatched from the east and west
and settled into a can of pinto beans,
horses with bent backs
standing by their strong shacks
rotting but refusing to fall
because damn you it's all
I know and it's mine.

And we're fine.
Tremendous, even;
I've never felt better about
what we're all good god damn doing here...
Ope! End up, the can on the floor feeds the fear
that it would turn to worms on the page
or in the air and I'm so afraid

that I swear: I'll do anything to escape,
even crawl over you crawling over me.

How is it only 3:04p CT?
Maybe this whole zone is a valley,
Central, center of the
universe, watching it all
happen around us
wishing we were there;
At least then I could climb,
make the grade.

But it's not. It's a blade
of grass, cut plains and mole hills
I imagine are the mountains meant for me.

I've never felt so MT.

West, to Fake California MO

I wonder what that wood said
before complaining under my feet
standing over the antique vanity,
taking Tennessee orange to the sheet
Mrs. Paisley had given to me.

It shouted, "PROUD TO BE A PINTO!"

If I could hold that feral moment,
I'd like to think I wouldn't
continue to scrawl "WILDCAT"
in 7-year-old screaming uncontrollable crayola wax,
sowing broken McDonald's happy meal
transformer toy minefields

and instead search
Grandma Bayne's silk drapes,
broken windowsill,
brass photoframes,
porcelain free-standing tub,
old tile undiscovered and mil-

-do whatever it took
to make them home.

Our Zone

for Joanna

When I think of thoughtful,
I am full of her.
I'd feel foolish,
if she wasn't fuel of me.

Her kindness conveys
in the biggest small ways:
non-dairy, low cal, milkshake.
Googlotti giggles meet us untainted.

We've spent over
12 seasons building the code;
she smiles, "you has a wickedness in your SOUL!"
Part-time cruisin' to a broken
6-cd changing life she somehow chose

to love so much, she ordered two,
pure blonde daffodil and ocean water blue
rudey nudie goon bag attitude.
You're heaps mad lucky mate, to be one of her dudes.

Seizer

Caesar said,
"No one is so brave that he is not disturbed by something
 unexpected."
Cesar said,
"Art should disturb the comfortable and comfort the disturbed."

For most of spring,
Dad repeated to his son,

(while tilting at windmills)
"Jon,
(and his name is mine)
you can be right
or you can be correct,"
one of many statues erected
in principled halls,
hollownely.
He'd never known any
different; the strongest brick
lays by itself,
on its own side,
relying on no one
and nothing.
But can it be building?

When you said you can read me,
did you know
that some books are better closed?

That I shelter in your cracks
as my stunted roots grow
them apart, tendrils intending
slow at first but fantastic like beanstalks,
to show that although I am bound
I cannot be contained?

Did you see I am giants and hunger,
high fantasy and heaps of drama?
Did you want me small
so I would not be tall
enough to fall
to my
death?

Is that what you planned for me,
or was I at best guessed
in your cloud castle?

Old you, young you, past you
spoke through a stranger:

"Ironically a pre-ordained life can ordain free will,
being the only situation in which a person is truly free."

I looked at his profile,
and all I needed

was retweeted Ben Shapiro
to know this would probably
fall short of productivity.

But then I wondered:
if this man met me in the street,
would he see his little boy
weak and prodigal?

I'm glad you changed.
Nothing in my life has been immutable.
I'm not sure, but I am strong and probable.

I don't need to be wise
to know I wouldn't bend again,
wouldn't break so tenderly,
wouldn't say, "Uncle."
He doesn't get to run his finger down my spine
and thumb through my chapters.
He doesn't get to know what's coming.
He doesn't get to know how I end.

Call Away

Eyes close and cobblestone memories
abound, wrapped in past freedom, keys that opened every
 door in every building;
I stumbled over 5th Street, missing something owned but
 never mine.
Implicit permission, not temporary conditions, but did
 that translate to real?
Was anyone kinder, more confident, more understanding?
Were their lives longer, more intimate, more fulfilling?
Did unlimited doing bloom into more or less beautiful?

Eyes open and the interwoven finger moment
sneaks a tickled shoulder and spritely grin,
rapt in present freedom.
Our feet caught each other on Court Street,
and we were in a different time, maybe even place:
hoofclop progress, wild and dangerous,
leathers and lace,
belts and buckles,
reckless sweat, dirt, and effort;
fringe pheromones.

Light campaigned across your face,
bodies laying siege to the last minute.
If it had been a kingdom in smoke and long shadows,
we nearly fell into the tug
and made it our own.

Wife*

I spent all day
contriving dramatic ways
to describe how, who, what, where, why, when makes a husband
because I wanted the blood flutter again.

Names contain needing.
You don't need anyone.
You could do it all yourself.

So, my heart swells
that you ask your risk
and know hIgh am worth it.

Maybe I defined husband* in the rambling.
I think it's being proud to call you

Who
I
Find in
Everything.

The Wolf Who Cried Boy

It watched him return to the village,
incredulous but accepting,

and thought if only
it could smell like him
it could eat like him
could look and speak like him,

then maybe
it could sleep like him.

So it wandered in early morning
when the lowlight hovered
over its features
dressed best and groomed
for the future.
"Boy!"

Finally it was celebrated
and laid to rest.

Scotch Blankie

Sitting on the porch with MacGregor;
we're waiting for the rains to cascade.

He's cheap and doesn't like me
much in the morning,
but he's smooth and puts me to sleep
when no one else is around.

They're saying the Missouri might be 31.7 feet by the end
    of tonight.

I only have 2 and they won't get me any closer to you.

So, I let MacGregor put me back in the ground
where I cheek a velvet blanket that feels like you sound.

The Life of a Sideways Sunflower

It started the same as the others:
one of 22 seeds in a package sold for $1.93
at Schulte's on route C,
full of dry life
and photosynthetic potential.

Dirtbound is an odd journey in the prison tense:
potted, buried, stuck, and expected to change,
to be uprooted and make room for something else
while maintaining photo-genetic potential.

Don't we take it for planted
that re-placed sprouts tend
to survive our misplaced whims?
We should expect anything ripped
from the ground to succumb,
without the fortification of origin,
to pathogenic potential.

But this one especially was not supported:
coat shed,
roots exposed,
leaves left unfed,
taught the sun was sideways,
lied that its lot was crawling
like a vine in pantomemetic potential.

39

Until by nature of passing animals,
heaping hands,
the understanding
and overflowing of water,
and the knowledge that
it is just carbon dioxide
and bad timing,

it found a powerful name in solid, settled soil
and even a stabilizing rock or three.

Instead of a tall lamentation,
it is a reminder that all aggravation
only brings the flower closer
to the earth who holds her.

Who Pays Your Heartbeat Bill?

They closed up McCarty and West Main today
and canceled all the children's events.
No matter where we poured the blame or prayed,
higher the occupying water went.

Schroer cried, "I was able to walk there a week ago;
I should be able to walk there forever!"
like womb to resurrection he's Captain America Jesus Bro:
gotta be East High to think that's how it works.

The Governor said, "maybe if I
and my weathermen agree,
we can force the river to relent."
They made god cry in impotent ink
'cause they couldn't steal nature's consent.

Eidolon

For Damian and Jeremiah

I say,
"We are a family of the mind."
He replies,
"Life is a bad venereal disease."

Dame's the same sober or drunk.
Only difference is whether he sits or wanders

:THUNK:

bumping into flowertables,
bumblebee in ashtray pollen
dropping knowledge on
peoplepetals un-gently.
You only live by telling
comfort to go suck your dick.
Sleep, work, and fuck is not
what you want to build your idol on.

Nothing is an unguent,
like a 5-hour car ride
meant to take 2 this
crazy bitch had shroom
clouds had to ask who

Blew America Up
then refused to
apologize for the truth.
Baraka to the future
issues a Stern warning:
you gotta grease the cops
then they shoot your career
because they can eat fear.
Fuck you and the pigs
whose skin made the luxury seat
you rode in…idle on.

Sometimes, when we call a thing "New,"
what we mean is "no news are good,"
like who wants to live in Old Jersey?
I mean, who the fuck wants to live in new shirts
and take your fuckin' shoes off;
home is where your feet freeze
where your lips crack
where your hands split
where the monster chose me
and I put dreams into a needle.
She asked me why and again
I said, "who am I to argue when
it's right
FUCKING
THERE IN THE NAME.
IT'S NOT A WANTLE.

Who are my people?
Stomach boils;
it's not like I couldn't eat,
but I'm too busy chasing
the hallucinations that hunt me

when I hide alone.

Maple Molly Brown

His bicep cradles the dowel gouge,
a homemade animal learning
to shave the rough
and shape the flame.

How it glitters in the fluorescent bars
and hides in the leaning lamplight
appear
disappear
every degree slightly different
in the shape and hands of a skilled maker.

It'll sing through the stains of hide glue and varnish,
measured twice and cut countless times,
until imperfection becomes character
and all the work
all the loss
all the curves
all the grafted "mistakes"
from an overzealous maker
never changed how much love
is in bumbling, hated hands.

Unsinkable is a skill the master always had to teach.
"Jon, that is a beautiful piece of wood."

It was not spruce.

It always had waves, never smooth.
It marred saw tooth and broken blade
resisting change

but it had never refused.
It had waited a lifetime or two
just to look at you
and me
and say

"You choose beautiful wood."

Ein Bier Bitte

He was against us
with all the labels we used
in quiet consternation after class
stunned that he wouldn't pass
"We're doing all we can,
but he's obstinate," motionless:
pupil closed to the rest.

Fail him now or later;
it didn't seem like it'd matter
or that he'd care yet
we did justice.

Fighting until the end
we sat and stared
unaware of how scared
stone could be here and now
and swiftly thereafter.

"You're shaking...

...how can I help you
through this struggle?"

He'd worked 84 hours
by Thursday sleep was a dream

Life was death
was the Christmas present
enough to sustain missoery?

Forced, deliberate kindness
"I hope you feel better
and have a good day"
the last words I got to say

before rumbling inside
about how he had one more chance
in quiet consternation after class
stunned that he would pass
"We're doing all we can,
but he's obstinate," motionless:
pupils closed to rest.

Rule of Thumb

When in doubt, don't hurt children.

"But there were no children
or if there were,
they weren't harmed
or if they were,
we didn't mean for them to be
or if we did,
their parents should have known better"

than to stand just
on the other side
of a fence built so far
up our southern border
that it must plumb
have been made
to sit on and play thumb war.

One, two, three, four,
"children are a heritage from the Lord."
Five, six, seven, eight,
try to keep your story straight.

These Lyrical Bones

For Cass Freeland

Pages to ashes,
Ink to dust;
so all lyrical bones, victim to rust
must make their meter,
prone to the passing-over
of impatient eyes.

The eyes, I believe, are an acquired taste.
They should not be forgotten as opposed to the face, but
    cannot be fully trusted…
they speak volumes if you know them, yet otherwise unite
    in silence.

There are no maps between men and eyes.

Being so aesthetically ageless, they promise only for a moment,
petrifactively certified to bide the rhyming tide.

For they are the cream of the dream,
two drops of even
essence lopping off the
head of motive
instead of love.

But you wouldn't know
of what I speak:

the pillars that line the peaks and slopes of written hopes;
words that are bones, unbelievable until they slip
amidst your lips and pour so much more

than ashes and dust from lungs that
must exhale their life before
inhaling their worth.

Only then do they
fly from Earth.

Requiescat
in pace.

The Wound

I long to look at length, but the blemish will not fade.
If any change, it grows ugly in the weather of my prying eyes,
but my curiosity is not satisfied.

I reach for it as a child, in clumsiness and innocence
testing the purity of the wound:
detect no infection, but now it's open.

The most delicate of flowers - its petals spread wide,
welcoming the wasteland,
loathing breath and moisture, for all that is life stings

and all that isn't, doesn't matter; what creates can destroy.
And so, our sincerest of fingernail whims
stand in the way of healing when pain is the stimulant
and fear is not feeling.

How, then, do we know what is alive unless we kill it?
Attention, addicts,
peeling the limelight for citrus rapture.
Catharsis feels like stasis, baseless yearning.
But without vicarious charity, the venerable,
We,
cannot be, living in the disparity of ignorance.

Uncouth...
finally, we've found the truth.

Which is the sweetest sound?
The leading tone of which no living ear has proof,
or the absence, without which we are surely unwound?

Suppose that is the origin of curse:
I must always do more, knowing
not all ways can be done. So I toe the line
or sink ships in the dune, where only three things
   are shore:
death, taxes, and the wound.

The Charge of Laurens, 1782

> *"How strangely are human affairs conducted,*
> *that so many excellent qualities*
> *could not ensure a more happy fate!"*
>
> ~ Alexander Hamilton

Some things when taken beating
turn colors like changing seasons.
Green and black and yellow blue
taught to keep a useful watch
in case fall comes early.
I am so clumsy.

I had dreams, goals, ambitions
friendship, home, and history lessons.
My first nature was caring
but it became second
when he stole third.
I am so pretty.

I wanted no reward after you,
and few awards can show
how hard I've worked to do
more than you ever expected
and less than you would notice again.
I am so driven.

This heart when taken beating
never needed growing up.

Started purple, bruised and bleeding;
I don't need your fucking help.
Give me love and give me nothing.
I am so honored.

I will do this shit myself.

Magnum Opus

Mother said, "don't cause a scene,"
but my love for causes grew
to cartoonish reality.

She put her fear before me
and I never forgot, even
trying to wrest it from
her restless hands.

Dad didn't take shit
from anybody,
and spent his days
staying far from close.

He's my fucking hero,
and it makes me sick
that we are closest
when we are far.

Where they came together, I came apart.
Where they came apart, I came together.
Either way, I am a start forever.

To tell you the truth, I'd rather not be.
But as I am, not being would mean
The End.

And It and I
are sworn enemies,
so this will be the Life of me:

Being as I'm me
and all I do has meaning,
I will raise the Mean.

Recognizing the terrible wonder
in those deep brown eyes,
I will put Life before fear
and close before far.

Our soul is solely wanted,
making all the difference
to the naked heart.

When faced with the magnum,
I choose my Opus.

Puerto Rico

There's a money storm in my eyes.

Bounty mouths talk
about the eye as relief,
but I live in a house

   eyewalls
of eyefloors
   eyeceiling

open cup of coffee
still rejecting eyelids.

Having no scratch,
I start from bruise,
building myself
with broken light poles,
working without power,
expecting to be abandoned.

Those who could do didn't care;
those who care can't do – I
end up doing for them, too.

Proud and ashamed
tired and Nonstop
Full of empty

   I can't eat your paper towels.

Silence, Patience, Struggle

This was the poem thoughtfully
Unwritten
because you didn't want it.

So, I decided
to be here for you
instead of there.

Lockwork

We are Watched.

You can see on their faces:

Partisan pendulum
Ready to spring
Over cloudy crystal.
Band together
Layered in gear,
Every hand up
Making the Movement,

running in of time like battlelines in open field,
firing lies at history and wondering why this world we wield

feels empty.
Will we then Still

deny that the Skies
have their Eyes upon us?

The Eel Question

Grizzled men scoff
pulling carts and bags
near the edge of the duckweed
lake at Veterans Park.

"It's not algae. If you look
close, you can see
individual leaves.
You know why it's overgrown,
right?

Fertilizer flows
down the drainage ditch
from the country club."

Another spits,
"and these fuckin'
people catch the carp
that are supposed to be eating it.
Once saw a great big ol' one
just laying on the grass...."

I contemplate the curtain,
how it aggravates the throwers
who wish only to fish for discs.
What pastime would they have
if all their plastic always came back?

Would they miss their stories
of the schmuck who dredges
to sell their bad luck online?
Could they be so close
without commiseration?

Or do they need part of
anger to achieve anguilla?

Each one carries
their own eelings,
dreaming of Sargasso,
where they've thrown
the government,
common sense,
the youth,
God,
these days,
the one they wanted back,
and the dutiful loss
that allows this place
to keep its name.

Long-time poet and regular performer since April 2019, Jon Freeland has previously performed in three features in Belle, MO with the Osage Arts Community as well as being published in *Reported For Duty: Veteran's Anthology, 365 Days Poetry Anthology: Volume 3,* and *The Gasconade Review Presents: Strange Days, Stranger Nights.* He is also a host at the Gumbo Bottoms Open Mic in Jefferson City, Missouri. Father, husband, best friend, teammate, and Coordinator of Staff Support working with the Intellectually and Developmentally Disabled Community by day, he enjoys disc golf, gaming, music, candles, listening, ambiguity, puns, and aggravating the people he loves.